Thrive!

Thrive!

Succeed in Life—Let Your Spirit Come Alive!

KAREN L. BAZZLE

XULON PRESS

Xulon Press
2301 Lucien Way #415
Maitland, FL 32751
407.339.4217
www.xulonpress.com

Unless otherwise indicated, Scripture quotations taken
from the King James Version (KJV) – *public domain*.

Scripture quotations taken from the Holy Bible, New
International Version (NIV). Copyright © 1973, 1978,
1984, 2011 by Biblica, Inc.™. Used by permission. All
rights reserved.

Paperback ISBN-13: 978-1-6312-9875-2
Ebook ISBN-13: 978-1-6312-9876-9

Table of Contents

Introduction

WRITTEN TO ENCOURAGE the reader to spend quality time with the Lord, *Thrive* is designed to help guide you through various areas of your life and, hopefully, direct you to a deeper relationship with God. Each day offers a Bible verse, proclamation statement, steps to practice the new concept, and a prayer.

According to Dictionary.com[1], the word *thrive* means "to prosper; be fortunate or successful." Beloved, you are meant to do more than just exist—you are created to *Thrive*! May the thirty-one days you spend reading this book help you to not only change old traditions or habits of sin, but also form new godly behaviors and lifestyles. May your time be blessed as He transforms, challenges, and strengthens your spirit. Our world is constantly changing around us; therefore, we must understand the Creator of us all in order to *Thrive!*

Enjoy the journey...

---

[1] Dictionary.com online, s.v. "thrive," accessed June 2, 2020, https://www.dictionary.com/browse/thrive

You Were ALWAYS Plan A

For God so loved the world that He gave His only begotten
Son, that whosoever believeth in Him should not perish,
but have everlasting life. (John 3:16)

WHEN I LOOK back on my humble beginnings, I have
to smile at where I began and where I am now. Certainly, I
have not arrived; nor am I at the top of anything. However,
the Lord had such compassion for me and kept me alive to
do His will. If you think about it, our Messiah came to earth
inside of a humble young lady, Mary—not a rich, influential
family—and was delivered in a manger that was located
inside of a cave with animals. (If you have the pleasure of
going to Bethlehem to see the actual site, it is a cave, not
a barn like in American depictions). Mary was a teenage
virgin when the Lord sent an angel to reveal to her that He
found favor with her, and that by the Holy Spirit she would
carry the Messiah. Meanwhile, she was engaged, pregnant,
and maintained her virginity. You can imagine what others
were whispering about her. As a result, Joseph, her fiancé,
was going to put her away quietly (Matt. 1:19). Despite what
others said or did, or even her own emotions, **she stayed
on course**. Let's face it: not the most ideal situation for the
mother or baby. Nonetheless, from Mary's womb emerged
a wonderful loving Savior that was destined for greatness.

My mother was not married when she carried me, nor
did she visit a doctor until the delivery. There are plenty
of others who were not born in ideal situations or circumstances, but that **does not diminish your worth or value
to the Lord**. No pregnancy or birth has ever taken Him by

surprise—*He has a plan for each and every person*. Our souls are all golden to the Lord, and He loves us ALL! So much so, that he sacrificed His only Son that we may all live righteously and be reconciled for eternity with Him (John 3:16). Each and every person matters equally, and we are all part of His divine plan. **We were ALWAYS Plan A; there was NEVER a Plan B.** His plan includes free will. Race does not divide us. No finances, geographical locations, ancestral lines, titles, heights, depths, demons, or any powers can keep or separate us from His love (Rom. 8:38-39).

Proclamation: You can have confidence, dear ones, that He who began a good work in you will bring it to completion (Philipians 1:6). Jesus can use you if you humble yourself to Him and accept Him as your Lord and Savior. Consider making a vow to draw closer to the Lord this year, in spite of your beginnings—let Him use you in a mighty way for your good and His glory. Only He can give you total victory from your past and let you walk in freedom! Additionally, if you knew the Lord as your Savior at some point but went astray, seduced by your own lusts/desires, please rededicate your life back to Him now! Tomorrow is not promised to you.

Practice: Have you humbly asked Jesus to forgive your sins and received Him as your Lord and Savior? Have you said the prayer in the past, but since been persuaded to walk another path due to circumstances? Regardless of your family background or history, you must understand the Lord loves you the same as every other soul He has created. Are you letting shame, guilt, or anything else hold you back from His presence? He allows U-turns at any point in your life, as long as you are on this side of the grave. The Lord desires a relationship with you; He loves you desperately and wants to forgive you of your past sins.

Prayer: Heavenly Father, please forgive me for everything I have thought, said, or done against Your will. I ask Jesus to come into my heart as my Lord and Savior. I need You to wash me clean and envelope me in Your loving arms. Fill me with Your compassion so I can walk in love. Please forgive me for going astray; I surrender to you again. I accept that I was always in Your plan—give me the strength and confidence to accomplish Your will. Amen.

You Cannot Earn It

For by grace are ye saved through faith;
and that not of yourselves: it is the gift of God.
(Ephesians 2:8)

"I THINK I ate a cat," said pint-sized Brittany as she curled up in a ball on the floor, gripping her tummy.

Raising her eyebrows and trying not to laugh, Freda said, "At five years old, if you ate a cat, I think you would know it! So, what makes you think you ate a cat?"

"My tummy keeps growling and it scares me," Brittany responded.

Relieved, Freda offered a solution: "Oh, that is a simple one; your tummy is telling you that you need something to eat, silly! Don't be scared; let's get you something to eat."

Just when she thought her day of babysitting was going a bit more smoothly, Freda looked down at three-year-old Jordan's long face and his lips poked out as he muttered, "I am not like my sister Jasmine, she is more gooder than me. I am not sure Jesus will ever love me."

Freda was heartbroken to hear her neighbor's son think his behavior could somehow determine the amount of love he could receive from Jesus. Realizing that kids think and say the darnedest things, Freda called all the children under her care together to sit on the living room rug and decided to seize the teachable moment.

"How many of you know that Jesus loves you?" she asked the group. Of the two girls and three boys she was watching, only two kids raised their hands – Brittany and Chris. "Chris, why do you think Jesus loves you?" Freda gently probed.

"For God so loved the world that He gave us His Son. My mommy says He loves everyone so much that He sent His Son," he proudly responded, grinning as he thought about it out loud.

Freda pulled out her Bible and started reading Psalms 139:13-16a aloud: "[You brought my innermost parts into being; you wove me in my mother's womb... and you know me completely. My frame was not hidden from you when I was made in secret and intricately put together in the lowest parts of the earth. Your eyes saw me unformed...]. Jesus knew you before you were formed in your mommy's tummy and loves you so much. He wants a relationship with you. Nothing you can do or say can stop Him from loving you," she added.

"Does that mean I can do what I want?" Jordan asked mischievously.

"What it means is that your behavior cannot earn His affection," said Freda. "He loves you completely. We ALL make mistakes (Romans 3:23), but it's how we handle the mistakes that can make a difference. Ask Jesus to forgive you, and the person you hurt, and then don't repeat the behavior. God wants us to learn and grow."

"So, you mean Jesus loves me just as much as Jasmine and Brittany?" Six-year-old Isaiah lit up like a light bulb as he seemed to understand it.

"Of course, He does! And Jesus loves me as much as He loves you! He knows you completely! **Salvation is a gift (Ephesians 2:8), you cannot earn it**," said Freda happily.

Proclamation: Brothers and sisters, the Lord knew you BEFORE He formed you in your mother's womb (Jeremiah 1:5a). As the lover of our souls, He went to deep depths to rescue us from the bonds of sin and death (II Corinthians 5:21). What He accomplished on the cross should compel us to serve Him out of love. His love does not discriminate. He created *all* of us. He knew you from your mother's womb—all your days were written in His book even before they came to be (Psalms 139:16b NIV), and yet He still chose to love YOU!

Practice: In a performance-based world, we tend to think hard work will warrant a good job, so we can earn love and approval from our supervisors, families, and peers. **It is liberating to realize you don't have to be 'Perfect Patty' to earn His love, because it is NOT based on our merit or actions; His love makes you good enough and you don't have to change your eye, hair, or skin color to receive it.** Make it your goal to receive His love today. Tell a family member, tell a friend, tell a neighbor, tell a coworker, tell a stranger: "I love you with the love of Jesus, and there is nothing you can do about it!"

Prayer: Heavenly Father, thank You for loving me in spite of my shortcomings. Fill me with Your love so I can love others. Amen.

Out of the Mouths of Babes...

"Train a child in the way he should go,
and when he is old, he will not turn from it,"
(Proverbs 22:6)

AFTER CHURCH ONE Sunday, my five-year-old son, Chris, asked me if his friend Louie from Sunday school class could come to our house for a play day. I said, "Sure, if it's okay with his mother." With that, both boys energetically scampered off to get Mrs. Rodriguez's permission for her son to join my family for play time. To their delight, she agreed, and Louie came home with me and my two kids. This was no easy journey, since I was recently divorced and no longer owned a car; we were trekking it on public transportation. The good ole subway system can be trying with two five-year-old boys and a seven-year-old girl. The boys were playing with their toy cars on the seats and making cute little beeping noises as they crashed their cars together.

Once we reached my house, the children ran inside to their bedrooms to get more toys. To my surprise, little Louie came to me crying saying Chris would not share his toys with him. I darted right into my son's bedroom holding Louie's hand and explained to Chris that he could not invite someone to his house and not share his toys; that is simply rude. I left the room to go cook dinner with high hopes that he received my simple message regarding how to be a good host. Five minutes later I heard the boys arguing—well, mostly I hear Chris yelling, "No, it's mine, it's mine, that's mine too!" Of course, I went running into the bedroom to observe my daughter quietly playing with her Barbie dolls, and my son snatching every toy Louie tried to play with.

As a concerned parent, I tried to exercise patience, speaking clearly and calmly in an attempt to rationalize with my son. After all, Louie was his guest. "Chris, you asked for Louie to come over to play with you at our house. He is your guest. You have plenty of toys and you cannot possibly play with all of them at once. Please share with him."

My son grabbed as many toys as he could and promptly replied, "They are all *my* toys."

I took a deep breath, because I was getting ready to break it down in terms a five-year-old could comprehend, when my daughter jumped in with an authoritative voice. "Chris, what about what we learned today in class, about the fruit of the Spirit? What about love, joy, peace, patience, kindness...?" (I think that is all she remembered.)

My son thought for a second, then let go of his tight grip on the toys and said to my daughter, "Yeah, you are right." He started handing Louie some toys and they went on to play very well together. I was dumbfounded!

Proclamation: I tried to rationalize with a five-year-old, and he responded better to a lesson he learned in Sunday school. My daughter shared what she knew of the Word of God, and my son immediately responded—why hadn't I thought of that?

Practice: Needless to say, they both taught me a lesson on how to apply the Word to my life in order to help others. It gave me a deeper understanding of what it means to "train a child up in the way that he should go" and how important it is to take children to church, read the Bible with them, and model the behavior before them. Are you modeling the behavior for your spouses, kids, grandkids, neighbors, co-workers?

Prayer: Heavenly Father, empower me to be a model of You and walk in love. I want others to look at me and see Jesus, even before I open my mouth with words of wisdom. Show me how to apply the Word of God to my life, so I can encourage others. Amen.

Folded Cloths

And the napkin, that was about his head,
not lying with the linen clothes,
but wrapped together in a place by itself.
(John 20:7)

RECENTLY, WHILE I was reading about Christ's resurrection in the Gospel of John, I noticed in the passage that the burial cloth that covered His head was folded. I never noticed this before. It is, nonetheless, an interestingly small detail that was worth investigating. John 20:7 tells us that the napkin, which was placed over the face of Jesus, was not just thrown aside like the grave clothes. The Bible takes an entire verse to tell us that the napkin was neatly folded and was placed by itself.

The book of John records that early Sunday morning, while it was still dark, Mary Magdalene came to the tomb and found that the stone had been rolled away from the entrance. She ran and found Simon Peter and the other disciple, the one whom Jesus loved. Mary said, "They have taken the Lord's body out of the tomb, and I don't know where they have put him!" Peter and the other disciple ran to the tomb to see. The other disciple outran Peter and got there first. He stopped, looked in, and saw the linen cloth lying there, but he didn't go inside.

Then Simon Peter arrived and went inside. He also noticed the linen wrappings lying there, while the cloth that had covered Jesus's head was folded up and lying to the side by itself, away from the grave clothes. Was that important? Absolutely! It is really significant? You betcha! Here's why.

In order to understand the significance of the folded napkin, you have to understand a little bit about Hebrew tradition of that day. The folded napkin had to do with the Master and Servant relationship.

> *When the servants set the dinner table for the master, they made sure that it was exactly the way the master wanted it. The table was furnished perfectly, and then the servant would wait, just out of sight, until the master had finished eating – the servants would not dare touch that table until the master was finished.*

> *When the master was done eating, he would rise from the table, wipe his fingers, his mouth and clean his beard, then wad up the napkin and toss it onto the table. The servant knew that this was a signal that means they could now clear the table. For in those days, a wadded napkin meant, "I'm finished." But, if the master got up from the table, and folded his napkin, and laid it beside his plate, the servant would not dare touch the table, because – the folded napkin meant, "I'm coming back," (*Bivin, Christ Linen Napkin).[2]

Proclamation: Our Savior left a beautiful message for all of us in that seemingly small gesture: He is coming back! Hallelujah!

---

[2] Bivin, David, N., "Christ's Linen Napkin (John 20:7)." *Jerusalem Perspective*, October 7, 2007. *https://www.jerusalemperspective.com/3878*

Practice: Beloved, do you see how detailed Jesus was in leaving a firm message that He is indeed coming back for His bride? Do you understand His detailed gesture of love to the whole world? There is no reason to ever doubt Him. Show His love with sincere enthusiasm to everyone.

Prayer: Heavenly Father, I appreciate how Jesus was so detailed in His message to affirm that He is truly coming back for His bride! I want to be ready and help others to prepare. Amen.

Commitment

Commit your ways to the Lord, trust also in Him,
and He will bring it to pass.
(Psalms 37:5)

COMMITMENT IS DIFFERENT from involvement. Involved means that you helped. Committed means you do everything you can to ensure success. To quote retired U.S. Air Force General Michael V. Hayden, "In an egg and bacon breakfast, the chicken is involved, the pig is committed."

Leaders fully believe in their cause and give their all. Their dedication and steadfastness are palpable to everyone around them. It is almost contagious! Ask yourself: are you a lover or a warrior? Lovers make better warriors simply because they are willing to die for the person they love. Although every warrior is trained to fight, he/she is not always committed to the reason for the battle. This affects performance. Not every lover is always a warrior, and not every warrior is always a lover. However, we can strive to be both.

Getting involved in positive activities can mean just going through the motions with no real obligations or emotional attachments. Believers/leaders will recognize wrong motives and provide counsel for reconciliation. Commitment is a heart thing. It is what drives you. It is passion. It determines what you do with your energy and behavior. Use this zeal to pursue a fervent relationship with the Lord. He is the personification of commitment. He exemplifies righteous excitement. Let Him fill you with a hunger and thirst that will encourage decisive devotion. Once your Godly passion is revealed, follow it! Never, ever give up!

> Commit your ways to the Lord, trust also in Him,
> and He will bring it to pass. (Psalms 37:5)

Discipline drives determination. Submit to the Almighty with your whole heart and let Him establish your ways. With the Lord, you are not giving up a lot; instead, you are gaining everything. Abba God puts dreams inside of you. He wants to help you pursue love and heaven, to name a few. Yes, that means you have to trust Him. Trust means having full confidence that He is who the Bible declares Him to be. It may not be instant, but as you develop a relationship with Him you will believe. Dedication to Him means not going by what you see with your eyes, but what you know in your heart. Jesus warned us against those who waver with the trends of the world:

> No one, after putting his hand to the plow and
> looking back, is fit. (Luke 9:62)

He is referring to the condition of their heart. They turn their head back because they begin to doubt and question things that are unfamiliar, so they look in reverse at what they already know—even if it did not work for them, it is familiar. They turn their eyes from of the Lord and onto yesteryears, allowing their past to keep them in bondage. You cannot have one foot in the church and one foot in the world—you are either *in*, or you are *out*. There is no in-between or neutral ground. You are committed to the Lord, or you are not. It really is that simple.

Proclamation: Commitment starts in the heart. Believers help others to pursue their godly passion.

Commitment

Practice: Read I Kings 8:61 on commitment; what does that mean to you? Have you ever given up on something that was important to you? Why? What drives you?

Prayer: Heavenly Father, help me to establish a committed relationship with You, and teach me righteous discipline. I am determined to pursue my godly passion and refuse to give up no matter the opposition. I look forward to our journey. Amen.

Thrive

AND HE TOOK the blind man by the hand and led him out of town. And when He had spit on his eyes and put His hands upon him, He asked him if he saw anything. And he looked up and said, "I see men as trees, walking." (Mark 8:23, 24)

When I wake up in the morning, I try to have a smile on my face and a grateful heart unto the Lord. Despite my attitude, I am not able to see the world clearly with my physical eyes; so, like many others, I must wear bifocal corrective lenses. If I let the glasses remain on my dresser and do not put them on my face, then my vision is blurry and limited. However, when I wear the glasses properly, I can see crystal-clear.

When challenges come our way, worldwide or personal, we need to keep the problem-solver (the Lord) in focus. If we concentrate on the global tribulations, financial complications, or other obstacles, we will become bogged-down and unable to comprehend or realize how God can use the circumstances to teach and/or elevate us. Just like putting on glasses improves our natural vision, putting on our spiritual armor (Eph. 6) will help us stay focused on the Lord! Don't ignore what's going on; just choose to focus on the Lord, who can provide clarity.

> "...when He (Jesus) spit on his eyes and put His hands upon him, He asked him, "Do you see anything?" (Mark 8:24).

Jesus touched a blind beggar who wanted to see, but did something unusual—first, He spat on the beggar's eyes, then put His hands on Him. We don't usually think of the Savior spitting on someone, an act that is considered unclean. Second, Jesus asked the beggar if he could see anything. I never saw another instance of Jesus questioning someone *after* He laid hands on them. This part gets misinterpreted a lot. Some say healing comes in stages, but I believe the blind man's response is the key to understanding the Lord's actions on that day. The Bible says the beggar looked up and said he sees people, but like trees, walking. That statement reveals that his spiritual sight was being reestablished first, then the natural sight clarified.

Proclamation: Beloved, your DNA is in your salvia! When Jesus spat on the beggar's eyes, He placed His life-giving genetic material on an area that no longer functioned properly for the blind man. With Jesus's DNA, the beggar's eyes had no choice but to thrive!

Practice: Is there a situation, worldwide or personal, that needs prayers? To what or whom will you choose to focus your attention while processing the circumstances? As a believer, will you choose to trust your loving Savior, who resides inside of you? Apply the life-giving genetic material that lives in you to any area not performing its purpose.

Prayer: Heavenly Father, I look to you as the problem-solver. I submit my life, my soul, and the following situation to You: (_____). I speak supernatural life to that situation (_____), both spiritually and naturally. My focus is on You, for I desire to thrive and please You. Amen.

You Are Handsome/Beautiful

God created mankind in his own image,
in the image of God he created them;
male and female he created them.
(Genesis 1:27)

IN A WORLD where physical beauty is splattered across television, billboards, social media outlets, and the internet, inspiring lust in many, it continues to lure men and women into a desperate trap of deception and confusion. Men are encouraged to pump iron to create ripples of muscles and use drugs for energy, while women are coaxed into plastic surgery and engage in tasteless diets to stay young-looking. Why? All in an effort to live up to the ideals of an immodest world. As a result, traditional male, female, and family concepts have been redefined outside of the Bible. Beloved, that is not God's best for anyone.

David records in Psalms 139:14, "I praise you because I am fearfully and wonderfully made; your works are wonderful, I know that full well." We are fearfully and wonderfully made by the Lord—He knows what He is doing with our bodies. He does not make mistakes. "We are God's masterpiece. He has created us anew in Christ Jesus, so we can do the good things he planned for us," (Ephesians 2:10). The more intimate our relationship with the Lord, the more we are transformed from the inside out. Too many receive the deceptive messages from the enemy because they limp through their lives starved for love and acceptance. "God is not the author of confusion, but of peace..." (1 Corinthians 14:33).

Beloved, let the Lord's love surround you in the radiance of His glory. He formed each and every one of us, and made us all special in His sight. All He requires from us is to yield to His creative work, without opposition or haste. Let His love for us set the pace for an amazing life.

Proclamation: What makes a person handsome or beautiful? Clearly, the heart: "But the LORD said, ...The LORD does not look at the things people look at. People look at the outward appearance, but the LORD looks at the heart" (I Samuel 16:7). The Lord has made everything beautiful in its time, (Eccles. 3:11), so trust Him and what/who His word says you are. Don't believe the misguided hype of the world; instead, submit to God. Resist the devil in the name of Jesus, and he will flee (James 4:7).

Practice: Bring the Lord your sacrifice of time and track how He blesses you and your family. Spend quiet moments before Him that will transcend time and transform your perceptions. Beloved, what stops you from spending time with God? Remove the hindrances and make God the priority.

Prayer: Heavenly Father, I desperately want to believe Your Word, which states I am handsome/ beautiful in your sight. Help me to overcome my struggle with grasping that You love me unconditionally. I am who Your Word says I am. I resist the deception from the enemy that tries to cause chaos and disorder within me and my family. Thank You for holding my hand while I pledge my childlike trust in You. Amen.

Spiritual Snipers

> For the weapons of our warfare
> are not carnal but mighty through God
> to the pulling down of strongholds.
> (II Corinthians 10:4)

WE LIVE IN a world where so many people live in fear—fear of getting deadly viruses or diseases, fear of losing our jobs, fear of not protecting our children, fear of global pandemics, etc... the list is endless. These strongholds paralyze and grip too many in their minds, which results in a huge surge of anxiety, panic attacks, or suicide.

It is important to realize that our reaction to life events will determine our future. The enemy's greatest weapon is fear. If he can get us caught up in our circumstances and emotions, we will fall into a downward spiral of self-pity and defeat. This leads to employment absenteeism and multiple visits to the doctor to mask or medicate our disquieted symptoms, which affect all our relationships. The Apostle Paul wrote in 2 Corinthians 10:4, "For the **weapons** of our warfare are not carnal but mighty through God ..." The word "weapons" is written in the plural form, since no soldier goes to battle with only one.

1. Let's start with knowledge of the Bible (yes, that means we have to study it, not just casually read it). To further convince you, Hebrews 4:12 states, "For the **word of God** is alive and active. Sharper than any double-edged sword, it penetrates even to dividing soul and spirit,

joints and marrow; it judges the thoughts and attitudes of the heart." Of course, Scripture gives us more aggressive offensive weapons to use, and we need all the weapons in our arsenal.

2. Plead (declare) the **blood of Jesus** over our lives, including our minds: "Having therefore, brethren, boldness to enter into the holiest by the blood of Jesus" (Hebrews 10:19). As the old hymn echoes, "there is power, power, wonder working power in the precious Blood of the Lamb."

3. Operate in the confidence that God loves us and is always with us: "For God has not given us a spirit of fear, but of power and of love and of a sound mind" (2 Timothy 1:7). Don't get it twisted; God is continuously with His people. His word tells us that He will never leave us or forsake us (Hebrews 13:5).

4. Quite simply: **Prayer.** "Praying always with all prayer and supplication in the Spirit and watching thereunto with all perseverance and supplication for all saints," (Ephesians 6:18). Beloved, prayer is a major part of the armor of God, and often a neglected weapon! We have to get beyond the beg and plead mentality with God to meet our wants—"God please give me... my children need... and bless..." It is in times of challenges, frustrations, health crises, etc., that we need to allow the Holy Spirit to pray through us the will of the Father. He may choose to reveal it to us so we can pray in our human language, or He may choose to pray through us with the gift of tongues.

Proclamation: As a spiritual sniper, we have to recognize the adversary's centralization of terror in specific regions (locally and globally), to locate strategic features in his attempt to release panic and fear on everyone he can. He is a liar and the father of lies, so we must engage our offense.

Practice: We must equip ourselves with the spiritual armor of God (Ephesians 6:10–18): securely clasp the Helmet of Salvation to cover our minds; firmly fasten the Breastplate of Righteousness to protect our hearts; strap on the Belt of Truth around our waist; Walk uprightly in the Gospel of Peace; safeguard the Sword of the Spirit, and confidently raise the Shield of Faith to thwart the fiery darts of the enemy.

Prayer: Heavenly Father, I worship You. Your Word says the prayers of the righteous avails much, so I thank You in advance for revealing the tactics of the enemy. I am spiritually armed and ready to act upon Your directive. I await your marching orders. Amen.

Can These Bones Live?

> I felt the power of the Lord on me,
> and he brought me... the middle of a valley....
> Then He asked me, "Can these bones live?"
> I answered, "Lord God, only you know."
> (Ezekiel 37:1-3)

THE LORD TOOK Ezekiel to the middle of a valley. I found this point rather interesting and almost odd. Why a valley? The valley is where battles take place, in the flesh and spirit. David victoriously fought Goliath in the Valley of Elah (I Sam. 17:19). In the Old Testament, battles typically took place with the opponents on each side of a valley. The Lord was trying to make a point here. Ezekiel saw that the valley was full of very dry bones, which represented death to masses (not just a few). How many of us are stuck in a rut? How many of us have given up on situations, opportunities, or relationships? Please pay attention to the fact that the Spirit of the Lord brought the prophet to this place to see something special, something spectacular.

Once the prophet was there, the Spirit of the Lord led him around the bones and then proposed what appeared to be a simple question: "Can these bones live?" When the Lord asks a question, is it not because He does not know the answer; instead, it is to make the receiver think a little deeper, beyond the obvious. At this juncture, Ezekiel was at a point in his journey with the Lord that he answered very tactfully and puts the ball back in God's court. The prophet addresses God personally with "Adonai, only you know." Ezekiel was careful not to doubt or hinder the Lord's will;

nor did he answer based on what his natural eyes could behold. Beloved, do not be limited by worldly cares or circumstances. I am not suggesting that you ignore them or act like they do not exist—I am merely recommending that you concentrate more on the Problem Solver than the problem(s). Adonai is our hope and our future.

Proclamation: The Lord goes on to tell Ezekiel to prophesy to the bones so they may live, and he obeys (vs. 4-8). Something spectacular began to happen right in front of the prophet—the bones began to rattle, and flesh was formed, then a covering of skin. The Lord performed a supernatural miracle after the man of God spoke life. The Lord could have achieved this phenomenon on His own; He did not need Ezekiel to do it, but He chose to work it through the prophet. Why? Unquestionably to show Ezekiel that ALL things are possible through Him. Can you imagine being privy to such a magnificent sight? His mind had to be blown; I was awestruck just reading it!

Practice: You are empowered with the same Spirit of God. What is around you that you need to speak words of life to? Beloved, speak authoritative words of life to your circumstances, opportunities and relationships! Not hocus pocus or cute little words—declare the words that God gives you and expect change.

Prayer: Heavenly Father, I stand firm on Your Word. I speak to my situation (_____) and declare LIFE! I know all things are possible to them that believe and are called for your purpose through Christ. I expect change, regardless of what I see. I thank You in advance for preparing my heart and circumstances for Your answer to my prayer. Amen.

Sounds

He answered, "I tell you, if these were silent,
the stones would cry out."
(Luke 19:40)

AS A CHILD, I can remember closing my eyes on a warm summer day and crouching on my knees in the thick grass to hear the sound of a creek swishing through my neighborhood. The water announced itself as it splashed through the meandering region near my house. Regardless of my neighbor's chatter or dogs barking, I could still identify the rushing or trickling sound of the creek.

Interestingly, quantum physics supports the concept of nature having a distinctive sound. It tells us that everything in our universe has energy that vibrates. Nothing is at rest—that includes nature. Water, trees, rocks, etc. ALL vibrate at varying frequencies. Vibration makes a sound; therefore, nature is speaking at all times. What it is saying? Would we ever be able to recognize its language and comprehend the message? Whether it is the resonance of the surging water, the strength or refraction of the trees, or the power and intensity of the rocks, nature firmly expresses its majestic allegiance to her Creator. What are we communicating as humans? Are we praising the Creator?

The apostle Luke records in chapter 19 (verses 37 through 40) a scene where Jesus was traveling on a never-before-ridden donkey colt into Jerusalem:

> "As He was drawing near – already on the way down the Mount of Olives – the whole multitude of His disciples began to rejoice and praise God with a loud voice for all the works they had seen, saying "Blessed is the King who comes in the name of the Lord! Peace in heaven, and glory to the highest!" And some of the Pharisees in the crowd said to Him, "Teacher, rebuke your disciples." He answered, "I tell you, if these were silent, the stones would cry out."

The disciples were filled with such joy as Jesus entered Jerusalem that it was hard for them to contain it, and Jesus knew it was improper to try to repress it. The stones will praise Yahweh because that is what they have been created to do. Do not miss the little nugget in the colt: he maintained a peaceful demeanor in reaction to Jesus's loving character and willingly carried the Messiah. It can easily take up to two years or so to teach a colt to transport a passenger, yet he immediately submitted to the Lord without any detailed incidents.

Proclamation: Animals and nature obey and praise the Lord. Can you think of any reason to give thanks and praise to the King of Kings? If you have breath in your body, limbs that work, and a sound mind, you have plenty of reasons to give thanks to the Lord!

Practice: Everyday, please examine your life to see the many blessings the Lord has bestowed on you and take quiet moments of time to express your gratitude to our Creator. Whether it is singing, dancing or simply lifting up your arms and voice to make a joyful noise—get your praise on!

Prayer: Heavenly Father, I praise Your holy, matchless name! I thank you for ALL of my blessings: _____, _____,

_____ and _____ (please list your blessings). I thank You for lovingly dying on the cross for my sins. You sacrificed Yourself for whosoever would believe, and I truly believe! I want to have a grateful heart, pliable with an appreciative and pleasant disposition filled with your compassion. I love you so! Amen.

Mobility

Finally, all of you, be like-minded, be sympathetic,
love one another and be compassionate and humble.
(I Peter 3:8)

WE LIVE IN a very mobile society, where most of us cannot imagine life without our cell phones. We feel the need to be in constant contact with others, so we do not miss a beat! Out of courtesy, we have resorted to using our thumbs to text our love ones when we are in a "quiet zone," so we do not further disturb anyone's peace (by talking on the cell phone) around us. Additionally, some will use their phones to Skype or take selfies to show pictures of themselves to others in real-time. We are so busy attempting to stay connected.

What was society like back in Jesus's time when there were no telephones? Oh wait, they actually spoke to others in person! People have always been very interested in fellowshipping with those who share similar beliefs. For example: I hosted two graduation parties, one for each of my daughters (Brittany and Jasmine) who both received college degrees. As I ushered all the guests to the kitchen, where I had prepared appetizer and dessert tables, I was astonished to observe their reactions. All the guests pulled out their cell phones to capture the decorations and food displays to post on Facebook, Twitter, Instagram, or some other form of social media to show others. I was simply amazed at the current standard of transparency and lack of privacy in which individuals choose to live. They feel the need to update their location and continuous activities to anyone who will watch and/or listen—why? Hoping someone will see their picture or video entry and solicit comments? I can appreciate their willingness to connect with others who have comparable interests or lifestyles.

As Christians, we should use this same drive to seek out those who are lost and show them the love of Jesus. "If anyone has material possessions and sees his brothers/sisters in need but shows no compassion, how can the love of Jesus be in that person?" (I John 3:17). Humans feel the need (with or without technology) to belong, to be wanted, and, ultimately, to be loved. That emptiness can ONLY be filled by Jesus.

Proclamation: We are so busy desperately trying to fill that void with people, actions, and performances to gain attention so others can relate to us. Our devices can keep us connected in various ways, depending on how we choose to use them. As Spirit-filled saints, we are His expressions and extensions of love. We are all born into sin (Rom. 3:23), so the only thing that separates us is being saved or unsaved. Heritages, customs, age, cultures, skin or eye colors, wealth, possessions, job titles, traditions, iPads, cell phones, and so on do not matter. We are ALL created in His likeness and image (Gen. 5:1).

Practice: While we have some form of mobility (technological and/or physical), please take the time to reach out with the good news of the gospel and love someone (using healthy boundaries) by talking and/ or texting some words of encouragement today. I challenge you to try to provide inspirational reassurance to those in the wilderness, since your messages may be the only parts of the Bible some folks will ever read. Don't miss out on your opportunity to be love in action—a simple smile or hug can go a long way!

Prayer: Heavenly Father, use me for Your glory by sending people across my path (online, in person, on the telephone, at work, in my home, neighborhood, etc.) so I can speak the good news of the gospel to them. I want to bless others and be an extension of Your love in action today. Amen.

Ability vs Availability

> ...the Lord saying, "Whom shall I send?
> And who will go for us?" And I said,
> *"Here am I. Send me!"*
> (Isaiah 6:8)

ACCORDING TO DICTIONARY.COM, "ability" is defined as a general word for power, native or acquired, enabling one to do things well. A talent is something that you are innately born with that just comes naturally to you, giving you unique skills and abilities. A talent can be strengthened and practiced. The Bible tells us that we are all born with distinct talents and gifts that set us apart from each other. With these talents and skills, we can do what we want. It's up to us how, where, or when we use them.

Meanwhile, our availability to be of service does not require anything special, just a willing heart. Our availability simply means the extent to which we are suitable or ready for use or service. We don't have to understand all the details; we just have to be obedient. Believers, who are chosen leaders, volunteer without hesitation, regardless of the cost or sacrifice, to get the job done with enthusiasm and energy.

Believers know that availability has nothing to do with ability. Having an inclined heart obliges the recipient to be cooperative and accommodating, even when it is not convenient. It does not require one to be ready, since that would imply preparedness. It is a condition of the heart which requires total submission of personal will. Believers/

leaders use their availability to tenderly surrender to the Lord's authority and comply with His plan. Those He calls, He qualifies (Romans 8:30), which means when He calls someone, He will provide them with whatever is necessary for success. We just need to heed the call.

For example, the prophet Nehemiah felt the burden of the Lord to repair the broken wall in Jerusalem (Nehemiah 1). He was a faithful cupbearer to the Persian king Artaxerxes. A cupbearer's job was to sip the king's beverage in front of him, and if he did not die, it was considered safe for the king to consume. It was a way to ensure the king would not be poisoned. The book does not say he did not have masonry skills, nor was he an architect. The book of Nehemiah does not state that the prophet had ever visited Jerusalem, either. He was simply willing. The Lord took a common man to do an uncommon task. The wall was repaired in a miraculous fifty-two days thanks to Nehemiah's willingness. He acquired the skills as he performed the task.

Proclamation: Believers make themselves available despite the circumstances. Beloved, we are *all* called to be servants. Our callings may not be the same, but it does not diminish the importance of each role. We are all members of the same body of Christ, who is the head of the Church.

Practice: Read Isaiah 6:8. Are you willing to go anywhere for the Lord? Are you depending on your abilities to carry you? What do your choices say about the condition of your heart?

Prayer: Heavenly Father, I ask the Holy Spirit to check the condition of my heart. Give me a heart for service and availability. I will look to You and not my own abilities. Use me for Your glory. Amen

Chalk Dust

> Create in me a clean heart and
> renew a steadfast spirit within me.
> (Psalms 51:10).

WE ALL KNOW rebellious people who try to do as much as they can without crossing the line. They get so close to traversing over the edge that they have chalk dust on their shoes. This same ashen powder leaves residue everywhere they go, quietly revealing their filthy footprints to others. What do your tracks disclose about your journey?

Frank Sinatra's "My Way" (written by Paul Anka) describes someone living life as they choose. Many people think this attitude is ok, but it is not. Trying to do everything our way is defined as rebellion. Proverbs 17:11 tells us that evil people are eager for rebellion. Our flesh does not want to come under the subjection of anyone's authority. People want to be their own gods. Believers/servants learn to respect authority and boundaries and teach others to do the same. We don't always know why or agree with limits, but we must trust God and honor the restrictions. Jesus did not die on the cross for our sins so we could disrespect or insult Him by living in darkness or total separation from Him. Instead, He did it so that we could be made the righteousness of God, while we were yet sinners (II Cor. 5:21). In the spirit of reconciliation, His actions show His love and obedience to the authority of His Father.

The Lord cares about our every move. Everywhere we travel leaves an imprint in our hearts, as well as on those we interact with. Boundaries are in place to help us, not harm us. If man is left to his or her own devices, he/she will pursue the evil imaginations of their own hearts (Prov. 29:1). Consequently, we need to pursue a repentant lifestyle. "Therefore, we must pay much closer attention to what we have heard, lest we drift away from it" (Hebrews 12:1).

Proclamation: Since rebellion grieves the Holy Spirit (Isaiah 63:10), believers/leaders leave out the chalk and stay connected to the right anchor—Jesus Christ.

Practice: Read Proverbs 17:11, which discusses evil people and rebellion. What does that mean to you? Do you see any chalk dust on your shoes? Are you willing to try a repentant lifestyle?

Prayer: Heavenly Father, cleanse me of my secret sins and thoughts. Give me a pure heart and clean hands before You. Help me to be quick to repent and lead others to You. Amen

Falling Leaves

The Lord changes times and seasons; He removes
kings and sets up kings; He gives wisdom to the wise
and knowledge to those who have understanding...
(Daniel 2:21)

I STEPPED OUT ON my deck yesterday to look at the
wooded area behind my house. It was quiet, and a slightly
cool breeze blew while I watched the squirrels scamper
across my fence. I noticed a couple of leaves that had
already changed colors falling off the trees and thought
immediately that the leaves are doing what they were created to do at this time of the year in Maryland.

The leaves flourish as long as they are connected to the
branch, which sustains their lives with nutrients from the
sun and the surrounding rich soil. However, interestingly
enough, once the leaves begin to change colors and start
plummeting to the ground, they complete their purpose by
providing nourishment to the same soil that once fed the
trees that fed the branches that fed the leaves.

This simple observation made me think about how
Jesus was sent to earth on a mission, trained others, and
then sacrificed Himself so that we could live. It also made
me wonder about myself—am I doing what I was created
to do in this season? Am I fulfilling my purpose?

Just as the leaf cannot grow separate from the branch,
we as believers cannot grow spiritually if separated from our
precious Savior. Jesus says that He is the true vine, and His

Father is the gardener (John 15:1); apart from Him we are unable to flourish and prosper. The Lord is the foundation or root that diffuses sap to the vine, and in Him all of our supports and supplies are met. Although there are many branches, there is one vine (Jesus) leading into the root. Believers are all one in Christ.

It is not so important how long we live on earth, but what we do with our time spent here. Ecclesiastes 3:1 tells us: "For everything there is a season, a time to every purpose under the heaven..." So clearly, we know that there are times and seasons for everything and a purpose for it all.

Proclamation: We need to look to our Heavenly Father, who controls the spiritual and physical seasons, to discern and recognize our current season and prepare us for change in the next. This recognition will determine our course of action, since we are required to do different things according to the specific amount of time we are allotted to complete our assigned tasks. We must then know how to proceed forward. "Even the stork knows when it is time to move. The turtledoves, swallow and crane recognize the normal times for their migration. But my people don't know what the Lord wants them to do" (Jeremiah 8:7 NIV).

Practice: Ask the Lord if you are doing what He has created you to do in this season. Timing is everything.

Prayer: Heavenly Father, seasons change—that is a fact of nature that You created. Things change all around us, both in the spirit and in the natural world. Help me to discern both the seasons *and* my purpose in each season. I realize You may require different things in and through me per season. I just want to be a blessing to You and those around me. Use me for Your glory. Amen.

The Power of Forgiveness

> As far as the east is from the west,
> so far hath He removed our transgressions from us.
> (Psalms 103:12)

I **HEARD A BROTHER** say how he held onto pain from his childhood. He gave his testimony as an innocent six-year-old going to the bathroom inside a church, where a man molested him. As adults, we tend to carry unresolved traumas or memories into our adulthood, not realizing it spills into all our relationships and making intimacy nearly impossible. We tend to put on a mask and/or build a wall of protection to survive. Let's explore common myths and myth busters:

> **1) MYTH**: Forgiveness means I somehow co-sign or minimize the offense. This causes us to go into a state of denial (like it never happened), and we internalize it. This fills your heart with bitterness or poison that prevents us from moving forward. Memories of abuse can terrorize our nights and paralyze our relationships with everyone. ("I just asked her to pass the mustard and she exploded!" We know that her anger had nothing to do with the mustard.) **BUSTER**: We must acknowledge it, process it, and turn it over to the Lord. Psalms 55:22 says, "Turn your burdens over to the Lord and he will take care of you."

2) MYTH: Forgiveness means the offense must be cast into the "Sea of Forgetfulness". We struggle with the "forgetting" part, thinking something must be wrong with us. For example, can a 13-year-old rape victim truly forget? Trauma does not go away easily. Micah 7:18-19 tells us the Lord will "subdue our iniquities and will cast all their sins into the depths of the sea." Further, Psalms 103:12 says, "as far as the east is from the west, so far hath He removed our transgressions from us." The Bible tells us in Genesis 4 that Cain killed his brother Abel; Moses killed a man in Exodus 2:12; and David killed Uriah in II Samuel 11. His ability to "forget" the offense of it is to release us from the penalty of it, because Jesus paid the price. We are being changed daily, more and more into His image and likeness as we yield to His Spirit. Sometimes distance is needed for us to have the fullness of forgiveness be manifested in our hearts. **BUSTER**: The Sea of Forgetfulness does not exist! He can not only take the sting away, but complete the healing to the point where we, like Joseph, can say, "You meant this for my harm, but God turned it not only for my good but for others."

Proclamation: The Lord wants to take the sting out of painful memories, so they can no longer control your emotional state, especially when recalling them. Chances are you will still remember it, but don't hold it over the person responsible. The Lord does not hold our transgressions against us, so we cannot either. Loving and forgiving allows us to walk in the fullness of mercy and compassion to be manifested in our hearts and experience.

Practice: Let me ask you this: what did the Lord have to forgive you for? How many times did you fall short? **I submit to you that walking in forgiveness is an act of submission to the Word and will of God that is NOT a one-time action, but a way of life.** *We cannot pick and choose who we forgive or what sins; instead, forgiveness goes across the board.*

Prayer: Heavenly Father, please release me from my prison; remove the pain and heal my wounds. Please help me to walk in forgiveness and freedom. I desire to please You. Help me to forgive _____ (you fill in the blank with as many names as you need to). Replace the pain with Your love and compassion so I can help others. Amen.

Steps to Keep Free

But love your enemies, do good to them, and lend
to them without expecting to get anything back.
Then your reward will be great,
and you will be children of the Highest,
because he is kind to the ungrateful and wicked.
Be merciful, just as your Father is merciful. Do not judge,
and you will not be judged.
Do not condemn, and you will not be condemned.
Forgive, and you will be forgiven.
(Luke 6:35-37)

JESUS BECAME THE ultimate sacrifice; He already died on the cross and paid the penalty of sin. So, let's explore steps to *keep* our spirits free:

1. CEASE ALL ACTIONS OR THOUGHTS OF REVENGE. Proverbs 24:19 tells us not to envy the wicked. The Lord's got this! Do not take vengeance into your own hands (Romans 12:19); instead, trust the Lord.

2. LOVE YOUR ENEMIES. How? Matthew 5:43-44: "You have heard that it was said, *'You shall love your neighbor* and hate your enemy.' But I say to you, love your enemies... Bless them that curse you and do good to them that hate you." Further: "If your enemy is hungry, feed him; if he is thirsty, give him something to drink. In doing this, you will heap burning coals on his head." (Rom. 12:20).

3. PRAY FOR THEM. Become burdened for their souls. "Bless those who curse you, do good to those who hate you, and pray for those who spitefully use you and persecute you, that you may be sons of your Father in heaven; for He makes His sun rise on the evil and on the good, and sends rain on the just and on the unjust. For if you love those who love you, what reward have you? Do not even the tax collectors do the same?" (Matthew 5:44-46). Sometimes a person is put in your path so you can intercede on their behalf. It will change your heart, impart compassion, and draw you and the person to God.

4. BE OBEDIENT. "Do not merely listen to the word, and so deceive yourselves. *Do what it says.*" (James 1:22). Most people don't like rules or boundaries, nor do they like to be told how to do things. Instead, they naively or arrogantly believe they know best. One the contrary—only the Lord can see everything, including behind-the-scenes actions. "Everyone who hears these words of mine and puts them into practice is like a wise man who built his house on the rock" (Matthew 7:24). Listen to His voice and His Word the first time to hinder or avoid delays. One person CAN make a difference. **Jonah's obedience caused a whole city to repent (Jonah 3)!**

Proclamation: Beloved, unforgiveness is a sin against the Word and will of God. "Forgive us our debts as WE forgive our debtors" (Matt. 6:12). Our forgiveness of others sets us free to receive God's forgiveness.

Practice: Why should Jesus forgive you, if you refuse to forgive others? As a believer, we should have His heart to forgive. There is joy in releasing His forgiveness! It sets you free. Don't let someone else's actions stop you from living to the fullest. Be free! Hallelujah!

Prayer: Heavenly Father, this is a new day that You have made; I will rejoice and be glad in it. Your mercies are new every morning. Please forgive me. Set me free so I will be empowered with Your strength to forgive and release others who have transgressed against me. Amen.

Tomb Dwellers – Redeemed but Not Released

And when she had thus said, she turned around and
saw Jesus standing, and knew not that it was Jesus.
(John 20:14)

SOME PEOPLE THINK It's okay to stay stuck as a tomb
dweller. Let's explore John 20:13-18, where the author
explains what this term "tomb dweller" means; these are
people who go by what they see and choose to stay inside
their pain because they feel justified, like they have a right
to be there. After all, they did NOT always ask to be there—
circumstances put them there. Are you a tomb dweller?

In verses 15-16, notice that Jesus came to Mary... then,
Mary made a pivotal turn towards Him, but failed to recognize Him. Jesus is standing right there in her midst, but
she was so caught up in her emotional pain, confusion, and
distress that she didn't even realize who was with her or
appreciate His words of life. Instead, she assumed He was
the gardener and asked about the body so she could be on
her way (a body that had already risen).

Jesus, in His love and compassion, got personal and said
one word: "Mary," She turned towards Him again, realizing
He was the Messiah. Isn't it just like Jesus to go to an intimate and peculiar place to reveal Himself?

Proclamation: Don't get so locked on your circumstances,
global issues, financial challenges, etc. that you allow them

to control your emotions and influence your actions. People can be bound by fear, unbelief, unforgiveness, diseases, pandemics, and so on; they can also become caught up in or controlled and overcome by grief after the loss of a loved one, or if their own vision of what their future should be has collapsed. They are stuck... they cannot move forward in life because they are mourning, surrounded and incapacitated by death. This can be an opportunity to look at the true-life source that stands before them with a future and a hope. He knows them and calls them by name to follow Him. Remember John 11:41-44, in which Lazarus came forth from the grave at the word of Jesus – "Lazarus, come forth!" However, he was still bound in the grave clothes and napkins, so Jesus said to "Loose him and let him go!" You want something different? Then do something different! Don't stay polarized—surrender and plunge into a loving faith-walk with Jesus. Guard you heart from anxiety, and trust God (Proverbs 24:3). Believe His report in spite of your circumstances.

Practice: The tomb represents death and grave clothes (bondage). Jesus is with you! Full knowledge of His divine presence can change your situation. You can be redeemed and not released. What area(s) of your life need to be surrendered to Jesus? What efforts do you need to do to get out of those grave clothes and walk in righteousness? Are your sins redeemed by the blood of the lamb? Do you know Him as your Lord and Savior? Beloved, build your faith up by reading the Bible daily, applying His powerful words, and walking in righteousness and obedience. Pray and pay attention to His voice.

Prayer: Heavenly Father, sometimes I need a nudge or reminder that You are always with me. I will look to You as my solution, and not dwell on my problems. I will speak to my issues and/or problems and tell them about my God! I want to be redeemed and released so I can be free to praise You and bless others. Amen.

A Place Called "There"–Getting an Answer to Prayer...

> "You have asked a difficult thing," Elijah said,
> "yet, if you see me when I am taken from you,
> it will be yours – otherwise, it will not."
> (II Kings 2:9-10)

SUFFICE TO SAY, many of us, if not all of us, have petitioned or asked the Lord for something (in the form of prayer)—whether it was healing for us or a loved one, salvation for family and friends, or perhaps a job and better financial management skills. Let's face it, even heathens are known to pray in a crisis. Sometimes these requests are met with an immediate answer, other times there is silence (delayed, but not denied), while other times it is simply no. Yet, there are those times when the Lord answers with a condition—you must go here or be there to receive your request. Let's explore the exchange in II Kings between prophets:

> ...Elijah said to Elisha, "Tell me, what can I do for you before I am taken from you?"
>
> "Let me inherit a double portion of your spirit," Elisha replied.
>
> "You have asked a difficult thing," Elijah said, "yet, if you see me when I am taken from you, it will be yours—otherwise, it will not." (II Kings 2:9-10)

Elijah makes it clear that Elisha's request is difficult, although not impossible, but he must be present or "there" with him when the Lord takes him. This made me wonder— where is my "there"?

Everyone is at a different place in their walk with the Lord, so the place of each person's "there" is going to vary. It is so important to be Spirit-led, submissive, and flexible. In doing so, the Lord is faithful to confirm things to us:

> As they were walking along and talking together, suddenly a chariot of fire and horses of fire appeared and separated the two of them, and Elijah went up to heaven in a whirlwind. Elisha saw this...and Elisha saw him (Elijah) no more. Elisha rent his garments in two pieces, then picked up Elijah's cloak that had fallen from him...and struck the water with it...it divided to the right and to the left, and he crossed over. The company of prophets from Jericho, who were watching, said "The spirit of Elijah is resting on Elisha." (11 Kings 11-15)

Elisha was told where to be —his "there." The prophets from Jericho confirmed to Elisha that he received his request. Where's your place called "there"?

Another example in the book of II Kings was Naaman, a prideful man seeking relief from his leprosy. "So Naaman went down to the Jordan River and dipped himself seven times, as the man of God had instructed him. And his skin became as healthy as the skin of a young child's, and he was healed" (5:14). His "there" was the Jordan River, as instructed by the prophet's directions.

Proclamation: What would have happened if Naaman went to a "cleaner" River, and not the Jordan? What if he went to the Jordan River but stopped after three dips? Would he have received his request? I think not! Or the blind beggar in John 9; Jesus, moved with compassion, spat on the ground and made clay from the spittle, applied it to the beggar's eyes, and told him to go and wash in the pool of Siloam. This beggar, who was blind from birth (vs. 1), made it his business to get to his "there" (the pool). As a result, he came back seeing. The answer to his request required an effort on his part.

Practice: How do we find our place called "there"? We seek the Lord with a specific request in prayer and listen for His direction(s)/instruction(s), which may come from the Holy Spirit, the Bible, or a man/woman of God. Your petitions will vary as well as His answers. Be diligent and patient in your pursuit. His power is limitless, and His solutions are boundless.

Prayer: Heavenly Father, I trust and believe you have all the answers. You are my source. Help me to willingly receive Your responses to my prayers and accept them, even if it means I have to go somewhere to receive my request. I seek Your grace and mercy, not to mention your answer(s). Amen.

Praying Before Acting

Early in the next morning, while it was still dark,
Jesus woke and left the house.
He went to a lonely place where he prayed.
(Mark 1:35)

JESUS WALKED IN constant communion with the Father. No matter what was going on in His life, He prayed (sometimes all night) BEFORE going places, making decisions, and choosing His inner circle (Luke 6:12); he also prayed for strength to endure. Jesus wanted His every word, deed, and action to reflect the heart of God—to accomplish this, He had to communicate with the Lord *daily*. Prayer is our communication with God. In the feeding of the five thousand and four thousand (Mark 6:30-44, 8:1-10), Jesus prayed for the food *before* passing it out to the multitudes until everyone was full, and there was more food left over than what they started with.

I watch so many Christians set out to do good things for all the right reasons, and then ask the Lord to bless it without ever consulting with Him first. They mean well, but we all know good intentions in our own efforts are like filthy rags before the Lord (Isaiah 64:6). Scripture tells us that Jesus separated Himself to spend time with the Father ahead of time so He could receive divine instructions, wisdom, and strength for all His assignments (not to mention how it renewed His mind and spirit).

Once we receive our assignments from the Father, we cannot always share it with others. In His darkest hour, prior to His ultimate sacrifice, Jesus asked the disciples to watch and pray **three times** (Matthew 26:38, 41 & 45); then, He chastised them for falling asleep. In spite of the disciples' best efforts, Matthew 26:39 records that Jesus "walked a little farther away from them, then fell to the ground and prayed." Jesus had to go a little further *by Himself*. There are times in our lives when we have to get **one-on-one with our Heavenly Father** without the support of our spouses, family members, pastors, etc. holding our hands. The Lord requires us to earnestly seek Him from our heart and the very depths of our soul—others, in their best efforts, *cannot do that for us*. We have to "work out our own salvation with fear and trembling with the Lord," (Phil. 2:12b). Jesus showed by example how we must seek our Heavenly Father for our daily godly direction, wisdom, strength, and endurance to complete the task(s) He assigns to us.

Proclamation: Only the Holy Spirit can equip us for our journey. Pray, talk, and listen to your Heavenly Father. Reading the Bible is great; it gives us insight into the past, present, and future as well as teaching the character of God. Please read it. However, more than anything, the Lord desires a *relationship* with you. Spend time listening and talking with Him. Let Him fill your cup daily.

Practice: Do you talk to the Lord on a daily basis? Do you have a relationship with Him? After giving the Lord your laundry list of wants, do you listen to what He wants to share with you?

Prayer: Heavenly Father, I desire a relationship with You. What does the King of Kings and the Lord of Lords want to share with me? I want to listen to the Creator of the universe. Amen.

There is Purpose in the Pit

Joseph's brothers saw him coming from far away.
Before he reached them, they made a plan to kill him.
They said to each other, "Here comes that dreamer"...
and they threw him into a pit.
It was empty, and there was no water in it.
(Genesis 37:18, 19, 24)

HAVE YOU EVER felt like no one understands you? Perhaps the Lord has given you some type of vision of something to come and no one shares your passion? Are you in a dry valley or lower in a pit where you feel lonely, confused, or abandoned?

Joseph is an interesting character who appears to fall victim to his brothers' jealousy. He is his father's favorite child because he had him in his old age. His father, Israel, makes it very known that Joseph is his favorite, and that sparks resentment and envy in his siblings. The Lord gives Joseph two dreams regarding his future, and he naively shares them with his brothers. In one of the dreams, his brothers and father bow down to him; needless to say, his siblings went from jealous to hateful, and plotted to kill Joseph. Sometimes the Lord reveals things that are for us, not to be disclosed to others. Not everyone can handle your dreams. This was only the beginning of his journey...

Joseph was **persecuted** by his own family! He was tormented by the very support system that should have been there for him. His own family called him names ("the dreamer"), stripped him of his coat, and threw him in an empty pit. Ancient pits were deep and narrow, filled with bugs (sometimes scorpions), and no food. Keep in mind, he did not do anything wrong. Then he was sold by his own brothers to Ishmaelites on their way to Egypt as a slave. You can just imagine the utter horror, betrayal, and abandonment he must have felt. However, in the midst of his **pain**, Joseph remained faithful and **persistent**. He did not wallow in despair or give in to depression; the Lord gave him **peace** to endure.

Just when he thought things would get better, he was sold to Potiphar, captain of the palace guards; not because he was bad or lazy, or because he'd done something wrong— just for money, to make a profit. Have you ever felt like someone sold you out/betrayed you for money or pimped your gifts? Despite all this, the Lord was with him and he was successful; the Lord blessed everything Joseph was associated with, and Potiphar saw the Lord was with him, so he did not withhold anything from Joseph except his wife. The wife began to desire Joseph and tried to seduce him. Joseph fled from the sin of adultery but got thrown into jail anyhow (due to the wife's false accusations). Even though he **practiced** righteousness, things for him went from *bad to worse*!

Proclamation: How many have had that experience? Once in prison, he was again granted favor from the Lord and, over a period of time, he began to interpret the dreams of the prisoners. Once the prisoners were free, one of them eventually remembered him and recommended Joseph to interpret the king's dreams. The Lord revealed the meaning of the king's dreams to Joseph, who shared it with the king. Joseph was then elevated to rule over Egypt! He went from *prison* to the *palace*! How?

Practice: The Lord **prepared** and **perfected** Joseph's heart for the task of saving his family, his people, and a whole nation from famine. Joseph was approximately seventeen years old when his life was abruptly altered by a desolate pit; however, the Lord would use this experience to give him **power** and authority over a mighty nation (at the ripe age of thirty)! The Lord uses all things for our good, just like he did for Joseph. Did his brothers bow down to him in the end? Of course, they did! There is **purpose** in the **pit**!

Prayer: Heavenly Father, I am determined to praise You despite everything going on around me. I need Your peace to reside in me. I know you are preparing me for my future. Amen.

Shifting our Thinking on our Journey into the Heart of God

Praise be to the God and Father of our Lord Jesus Christ.
In Christ, God has given us every spiritual blessing in the
heavenly world. That is, in Christ, He chose us before the
world was made so that we would be His holy people
without blame before Him. Because of His love, God had
already decided to make us His own children through
Jesus Christ.
That was what He wanted and what pleased Him, and it
brings praise to God because of His wonderful grace. God
gave that grace to us freely, in Christ,
the One He loves.
(Ephesians 1:3-6)

THERE IS A major difference between a person who
knows they are already approved of and loved by God and
someone seeking His approval. One experiences peace and
joy; the other unrest, strife, shame, and rejection. It takes
time in the presence of God, receiving His love, renewing
our minds, and having our souls healed to understand the
revelation that we are already approved.

This is our journey into the heart of God.

Because He loves us, He provided forgiveness and
redemption through the sacrifice of Jesus's finished work
on the cross. He is absolutely crazy about each one of us!
He knew it all before we were born and was relentless in His
pursuit to make us part of His bride. God's prophetic gifts

cause Him to see us in our end results. The Master Potter knows what He created each of us to be and is committed to getting us there.

Philippians 1:6 says, "Being confident of this very thing, that He who has begun a good work in you will complete it until the day of Jesus Christ" —in other words, He is fully committed to our journey. To lack understanding in this area drives Christians into religion and works—always striving to win God's approval and love. So how do we begin our journey? The adventure starts by surrendering and allowing the Master Potter to make and mold us. "We are like clay, and you (God) are the potter; your hands made us all," (Isaiah 64:8).

Proclamation: The greatest word we could ever utter to His will is *YES*! Our final sign of mature love towards our Savior is written in Song of Solomon 7:10, where it says, "I am my Beloved's and His desire is towards me." It means He longs for us. His concerns are what I care about most. His desires are my focus. My role as a lover of God requires more of me than a servant.

Practice: We have to shift our thinking from just being His servant to be His bride. His priorities are MY priorities. His heart of compassion is my heart of compassion. What moves Him moves me. "For in Him we live, and move, and have our being" (Acts 17:28). Beloved, let love set you free by saying YES today to the lover of your soul—Jesus!

Prayer: Heavenly Father, I say YES to Jesus! I want to be consumed with the cares of my precious Savior. I now realize You love and approve me as Your own. My desire is towards You. Amen.

Marking Time

"Brothers and sisters, I know that I have not yet reached
that goal, but there is one thing I always do.
Forgetting the past and straining towards what is ahead. I
keep trying to reach the goals and get
the prize for which God called me through
Christ to the life above."
(Philippians 3:13-14)

DO YOU FIND yourself frustrated that you have not accomplished all your goals? Has life thrown you a couple of curveballs? Have you made some bad choices for which you must now reap the consequences? How many of us have had to adjust because others have made bad choices that have affected us?

At the beginning of a new year, the gyms are filled with those who made new resolutions. When March approaches, the health clubs are emptying out again, and only the few committed remain. Most of us mean well when we set out to do things, but life happens. Simple things can be distracting, and we can lose our way; however, if we're not careful, these deviations can take us way off course and diminish our drive.

Proclamation: We can get side-tracked for various reasons, and then as we get older, we can become complacent. We settle into jobs that pay the bills, get caught up in the drama on television, and coast through our twilight years doing the bare minimum. We slow down, not realizing that we are getting further away from our God-given goals and dreams, and then eventually stop striving. We, quite frankly, just **mark time**. We don't do much of anything anymore, and if we do minuscule things, we just kind of go through the motions with very little or no effort.

Practice: Beloved, it is a new day in the Lord! I challenge you to check your goals and objectives and ask the Lord to prioritize your life. Turn down the plate, turn off the television, get off of social media, and seek Him for direction to get back on track. Shake loose those people and things that hinder your growth. Stop settling and start celebrating life! Don't just mark time; strive to ***move forward*** to accomplish His will in your life to reach your full potential. Your full potential will be so fulfilling for you. Spread Godly influence on others, enriching their lives. Beloved, thrive again!

Prayer: Heavenly Father, I thank You for waking me up and reminding me to thrive—to live life to the fullest in You. I believe You will put me back on track so I can achieve the goals You have for me. I want to finish this race, accomplishing everything You need me to do. I desire to hear You say that I am a good and faithful servant. Amen.

Laws

He saw the disciples straining at the oars because
the wind was against them. Shortly before dawn,
Jesus came out to them walking on the lake.
He was about to pass them by…
(Mark 6:48)

JESUS SAW THE disciples struggling, trying to do things
in their own strength. He watched them in their folly and
chose to go to them in an effort to help them.

When we have an assignment from the Lord, it can ONLY
be done with HIS strength, wisdom, and speed. We need
the Holy Spirit to empower and strengthen us. So many of
us look at our circumstances, use logic, and try to weigh our
options based on what we see, feel, hear, and smell, as well
as prior knowledge. On our best day, we are no match for
the Lord and His assignment/calling on our lives. We think
small (to be safe); He thinks BIG. We think down, He thinks
up. We think logical and impossible, while He thinks incred-
ible and possible! When He assigns us, He is aware that all
things are possible if we just believe.

It is interesting that a 747 Boeing airplane full of pas-
sengers and luggage can weigh up to 885,000 pounds and
still fly. The natural mind says it is impossible to get something that heavy to not only fly but soar above tall build-
ings and clouds. How is this possible? Thanks to the law of
thrust (one of many), a huge airplane is able to fly. Likewise,
Jesus walked on water right in front of the disciples, demon-
strating how spiritual laws trump natural laws.

Even in the midst of this illustration, the disciples were initially so caught up in their struggles that they did not see Him until He was about to "pass them by." Imagine that the Lord is right in your face and you cannot see Him because fear has gripped you. Why would He pass them (or you) by? As a gentleman, He is not going to force Himself or His help on anyone. If you are giving into fear (or whatever), you are allowing that to be your god—you choose to ignore Him. When the disciples finally saw Him and acknowledged Him, He stopped. Peter asked Jesus if he could walk on water to meet Him (Matthew 14:28). Such faith!

Proclamation: Peter knew he could NOT do it on his own, but knew it was possible with the Lord. After successfully stepping out of the boat (his surroundings/condition), Peter was able to walk on water! Sure, he got caught up on the sound of the wind and thunder, as well as the giant waves; then, he began to sink (vs. 30). In short, Peter took his eyes off of Jesus and back onto his surroundings. Don't be so hard on him; he was the ONLY disciple to experience walking on water. Out of compassion, Jesus grabbed Peter (who cried out to Him) to prevent an early demise. What can we learn from this awesome story?

Practice: 1) Your assignment from the Lord is based on HIS strength and wisdom—NOT your natural abilities. 2) No matter what happens, keep your eyes on Jesus! 3) No matter where you are in your journey, the Lord knows where to find you. 4) The Lord's spiritual laws supersede all other laws, so apply them to your life. 5) With God, all things are possible!!

Prayer: Heavenly Father, I know as Your warrior that I have an assignment from You. I must depend on Your strength and wisdom to accomplish it. I firmly believe all things are possible through You. I am ready to walk on water with You as I keep my eyes on You. Amen.

Sheep Without A Shepherd

My sheep hear my voice,
and I know them,
and they follow me.
(John 10:27)

I RECENTLY PONDERED THE following question: why does the Lord call us (Christians) **SHEEP**? Why not refer to us as beautiful peacocks? Fast cheetahs? It is interesting to note that the Bible makes at least 220 references to sheep (some are mentioned below). So, I did some research on the subject and compiled some facts about **sheep**:

"We all have wandered away like sheep: each of us has gone his own way..." (Isaiah 53:6)

"The Lord is MY Shepherd, I shall not want." (Psalms 23:1)

Sheep are not the most intelligent animals. Sheep are known to follow other sheep, even if it means the leader of the pack walks off a cliff to his death. All the other sheep will see this sheep fall to his death and go over the cliff anyhow! It sounds crazy, but they are known followers. In like manner, people tend to wander away from God, from everything that is right and holy. The wisdom of God is all knowing and all loving (I Corinthians 3:19), but many folks mindlessly leave the herd to follow a path to destruction.

Sheep need protection. Sheep do not have claws, sharp teeth, speed, or a ferocious roar to scare any predator away; instead, they are easy prey. They cannot climb trees, change their color, or even swim; therefore, they tend to panic when they are confronted with danger. Imagine what must have gone through the disciples' minds when Jesus told them, "Behold, I send you out as sheep in the midst of wolves" (Matthew 10:16a). The best move for a sheep is to stay as close as possible to the shepherd and remain with the herd. As Christians, we need to cling to Jesus!

Sheep make bad choices when they are hungry/parched. Sheep can graze peacefully for hours, but they become restless when food is scarce. Spiritual hunger occurs when we neglect to read the Word of God and fall away from attending church. Sheep need water and nourishment on a daily basis. The Good Shepherd "makes me lie down in green pastures; He leads me besides the still waters" (Psalms 23:2). We need the living water of the Holy Spirit continuously. A well-fed sheep will not be so quick to eat out of a stranger's hand, but a hungry sheep becomes despondent and impulsive. "Let me eat some of that red stew because I am weak with hunger... I am almost dead from hunger..." (Genesis 25:27-30). As a result, Esau gave away his spiritual birthright because he was desperate for food.

Proclamation: The Shepherd trains and disciplines His sheep to hear and obey His instruction. He is NOT the author or source of pain or suffering. He does not use the enemy's tactics to punish the sheep. The Good Shepherd never harms, breaks the bones, or approves of destruction. He uses the rod and staff to rescue and save. He goes after the sheep who are lost or injured from falling. He carries them in His arms and restores them to the flock. There is pain in this fallen world, and the sheep can get in trouble apart from the Shepherd. We can learn through our mistakes, and from difficult situations, because God turns everything for our good and adds no sorrow.

Practice: A wayward sheep's vulnerable heart can be forever changed, and his behavior can model devotion, respect, and compliance if he/she clings to Jesus. In short, sheep can learn obedience through discipline if they turn back to Christ.

Prayer: Heavenly Father, I realize I need to stay close to the Jesus Christ so I will not be vulnerable to diversions. Direct me, guide me so I will be obedient and abide in Your protection and encourage others. I will set aside time daily to read the Bible for spiritual nutrition. Amen.

Persevering... Without Family Support

> A house divided cannot stand.
> (Mark 3:25).

SIMPLY STATED, OUR families are being slowly seduced by the enemy! If your family does not support your Christian journey, just know that Jesus had challenges within His earthly family as well. We must stand in the gap for our families and children so Satan cannot destroy the very institutions set up by God to be a blessing. United we stand; divided we will surely fall.

The Apostle Mark records in chapter 3, verse 25, "If a house is divided against itself, that house cannot stand." We, the Church, have been sleeping far too long, while our families have been redefined by the systems of the world. In verses 20-21, we find Jesus entering a house, and again a crowd gathered, so that He and His disciples were not even able to eat. When His family heard about this, they went to take charge of Him, for they said, "He is out of his mind." Two issues here: (1) the crowd prevented Jesus from eating since they surrounded Him and obviously wanted to hear Him speak and perform miracles, and (2) at the same time, His family thinks He's crazy! Other haters accused Jesus of being possessed by Beelzebub, the prince of demons (vs 22). Have you ever shared a vision from the Lord and no one around you agreed or believed what you said?

Our families have been under siege! Ephesians 6:1-3 says, "**Children, obey your parents in the Lord: for this is right. Honor thy father and mother; (which is the first commandment with promise;) That it may be well with thee, and thou mayest live long on the earth.**" What we are actually doing: "*Parents, obey your children to keep them happy and provide all the material things they want to possess so they will not feel rejected by their peers and keep up with the Joneses!*" **It's out of order!** That's why our schools are out of control! Our prisons are overflowing. If children don't respect their parents, why would they respect anyone else? We want to label it ODD (Oppositional Defiance Disorder); I say call it what it is— "Lack of Respect for Authority or Rebellion Against God!" Since when is disrespect a disorder? We don't read about this in the Old Testament— why? Exodus 21:15— "Anyone who attacks his father or his mother must be put to death." Plain and simple! I'm not advocating the death penalty for children, but the need for **discipline in love** and respect; train them in the Word of God and teach them reverence for the Lord Almighty.

Proclamation: When we choose to make a stand for Christ, doing His work, our families may not understand us. There are spiritual Unabomber's who try to sabotage the work of God. Conflict is inevitable! Look at it as an *explosive* opportunity to learn from each other—teachable moments! Let's examine five fool-proof ways to bring families together:

Practice: 1) If you desire unity and harmony, then **speak truth** (Eph. 4:25). Don't practice deception! It causes division that can separate families for years! For we are members of one body. **2) Maintain self-control!** Be angry, but don't sin (vs 26 & 27)! Anger becomes sin when we attack the *person* and not the *problem*! **3). Be productive and share** (28). Don't carry members of your family; everyone has talents and skills to share with others. Each part of your body has a function that is important—the eye can't say to the hand, "I have no use for you" (I Corinthians 12:21). **4) Value each member of your family**, they are significant to their Creator. 5) **Show love and compassion** (John 15:12). Everyone wants to be appreciated, accepted, and feel a sense of belonging—especially from their families.

Prayer: Heavenly Father, please help me to not allow those who oppose me (even if it is my family) with their doubting thoughts or behavior to influence mine. Help me to stand on Your Word and not be a people-pleaser. I pray for those who misunderstand, misinterpret, and oppose the purposes of God for myself and my family. May they all receive Jesus as their Lord and Savior. Amen.

Thank God for the Wilderness

When Pharaoh let the people go, God did not lead them
on the road through the Philistine country,
though that was shorter. For God said, "If they face war,
they might change their minds and return
to Egypt." So, God led the people around
by the desert road toward the Red Sea.
The Israelites went up out of Egypt ready for battle.
(Exodus 13:17-18)

"WHAT GOOD CAN possibly come out of this? I don't like it! There are no familiar landmarks and it is completely unappealing to my senses!" These are words that might be shared by those who are sent to a temporary God-appointed wilderness. No one wants to be there; in fact, everyone is running to get out. Let's explore the Word of God to further examine the significance of the subject of the wilderness.

- In Exodus 3, Moses, at eighty years old, is called by God in the deepest part of the wilderness by a burning bush. Keep in mind that he ran there after killing someone.
- When Pharaoh said the wilderness has them closed in (Exodus 14:3), God used it as an opportunity to show His beloved people His mighty work, which served as a way of escape for them while swallowing up their enemies that would try to keep them in bondage.
- In I Samuel 17, David found the strength and courage to fight Goliath in the wilderness when his

brothers, who were trained in the military, would not do it.

- Luke 4 describes how Jesus overcame temptation after being led into the wilderness by the Spirit. Verse 14 tells us that He came out of the wilderness with such power and authority that many commented that "we have heard these scriptures in the past, but no one ever spoke like this before."

Proclamation: Why does the Lord send us into the wilderness? Exodus 13:17 tells us that as the Lord led His people out of captivity into the Promised Land, He did not choose the easier route where a battle would have taken place rather quickly, "...lest they change their minds." The wilderness is a place of preparation for divine purpose in our lives, a place to get us ready for battle. Exodus 15:22 makes it clear that even the bitter becomes sweet in the wilderness. You learn to trust in the Lord. Your faith will no longer be like a roller coaster; instead, it will be rock-solid. The old ways may look better, but we do not live by our circumstances (II Cor. 5:7). We learn to praise the Lord because we love Him, not because we feel like it. Additionally, Exodus also tells us that the wilderness was also a place of *supernatural* **presence:** a pillar of cloud by day and fire at night, bread/manna from heaven (revelation), **provision** (water and quail), **protection** (enemy destroyed in the Red Sea), etc. Through it all, God's **miraculous intervention**.

Practice: Remember, He always makes the way of escape out of the wilderness—it does not last forever. The Lord's people emerge out of the wilderness with the power, knowledge, and authority of God. Our very words can pierce right through people to their hearts. We should thank God for the wilderness and embrace His full will. Some of us have made several trips there, but the Lord continues to prepare His people. The Lord continues to work on our character.

Preparation is good when God is in it. I challenge you to the thank the Lord for the wilderness.

Prayer: Heavenly Father, I thank You for my temporary wilderness experiences. Although it does not always feel pleasant, I know it is for my good to prepare me for the work I must do and to help others. I know as I walk together with You, all things are possible. Amen.

Self-Perception

And those men gave the Israelites a bad report about the land they explored, saying, "The land that we explored is too large to conquer… we felt like grasshoppers, and we looked like grasshoppers to them."
(Numbers 13:32-33)

OUR IDEOLOGY ON self-perception will determine our behavior. The ten spies said "we felt like grasshoppers…" They saw themselves as very small and/or weak compared to the current occupants. We all have situations and/or problems that can appear to tower over us, with the potential to send us into a quandary. However, if we view difficulties as opportunities for the Lord to show Himself to us, then we can approach things in the spirit of love.

"We looked like grasshoppers to them," was the spies' perception of what they assumed the others were thinking. Beloved, do not look for validation, confirmation, or affirmation from others. God already told the Israelites that He was going to give them the land, so it was a matter of submission and simple obedience, not doubt and unbelief.

Submission is doing the right thing with the right attitude, while doubt and unbelief will stop you in your tracks and cause you to miss what is yours. As a result of what the ten spies believed, they said up front: "The land we explored is too large to conquer." Their assessment was largely centered on their disbelief and skepticism, based on what they saw with both their physical eyes and their (limited) spiritual eyes. As a result, they did not want to proceed forward to seize the land. By contrast, the other two spies (Caleb and Joshua), said, "We should certainly go up and take the land for ourselves. We can certainly do it!" (v. 30).

Proclamation: All of the spies saw the same land with the same occupants, so why were there two totally conflicting reports? Caleb and Joshua followed God fully, so they believed what the Lord communicated to the Israelites in advance and wanted to take the land that was promised to them; conversely, the other spies doubted and did not want to move forward with the plan. It really is that simple. Beloved, we need to see ourselves as the Lord sees us and follow Him fully so we can receive all of the things He has for us. We will all act on what we believe. Are you moving forward in Jesus because you believe everything He says in His Word?

Practice: All twelve spies saw the same things, but gave different reports; whose report will you believe? How do you see yourself? Do you listen to what the Lord is saying to you? What situation looms over you? How has your perception affected your behavior?

Prayer: Heavenly Father, I need a fresh perspective with Your eyes and Your vision for my life. I believe everything You say in your Word is true, so I submit to Your authority and Your will for my life. I know that I am a conqueror through You. I will act on what I believe in Your strength as you provide divine direction. Amen.

Prepare your Heart for Blessings

But My servant (_____), [can you place your name there?]
because he has a different spirit in him and has followed
Me fully, I will bring into the land ..., and his descendants
shall inherit it.
(Numbers 14:24)

HOW MANY OF us exercise our faith by praying for
something over a period of time, only to lose it (the blessing)
when we receive it? There are plenty of people who pray
for meaningful things with good intentions, like getting
pregnant or married or a promotion on the job— all are
awesome requests, since the Lord told us to be fruitful and
multiply (not to mention the companionship). What most
people neglect when praying to receive a blessing, though,
is **going beyond the wanting** and **ask for the wisdom** to deal
with it once they receive it. *With more "things" comes more
responsibility*. Success without obedience and the right attitude is a set-up for failure or an untimely fall.

For instance, Caleb was one of many spies sent to scope
out the Promised Land of Canaan for the Israelites—he saw
the same things as all the other spies, but he gave a good
report because he **believed and obeyed the words of the
Lord** and had the right attitude; as a result, the spies who
gave a bad report and ignored the words of the Lord (out
of rebellion and disobedience) were not allowed to enter
into the Promised Land. "But My servant Caleb, because
he has a different spirit in him and has followed **Me fully**, I

will bring into the land where he went, and his descendants shall inherit it" (Numbers 14:24). Are you following Him *fully*, with your whole heart? Half-stepping it won't work. Only offering the Lord a small portion of your heart does not change your nature or spirit. Beloved, your choices also affect your loved ones! When you make good ones, your family will inherit them.

Proclamation: We must ask the Lord to **prepare our hearts** to receive our blessings; in doing so, we connect our faith with His wisdom to bring honor to God. After all, everyone wants blessings, right? If the Lord gives it to us, then He wants us to have it—what we choose to do with it is another story.

Practice: Please be aware, dear saints, that we are held accountable for what we do with our blessings from the Lord. Bearing in mind that all blessings from the Lord are good, our obedience to His wisdom is key to keeping our blessings. "For I command you today to love the Lord your God, to walk in obedience to Him, and to keep His commands...then you will live and increase, and the Lord your God will bless you..." (Deut. 30:16). **Is your heart prepared for the many blessings your gracious Heavenly Father wants to bestow upon you?**

Prayer: Heavenly Father, I fully commit my heart to You. I seek Your wisdom to walk responsibly in every area of my life and what is to come. My success is fully dependent upon my attitude and obedience to You. I yearn for You to prepare my heart to receive every good and perfect gift You provide for me so I can bring honor and glory to You. Amen.

Saltiness

You are the salt of the earth; but if the salt
has lost its flavor, with what will it be salted?
(Matthew 5:13)

DID YOU EVER notice the more you eat sugar, the
more you crave it? Sugar can become an addiction that we
ingest in our mouths, rather than injecting it into our veins
or inhaling it into our lungs—therefore we don't view it as
harmful or habit-forming. If we choose to give up sugar, we
can get headaches, the shakes, and strong, uncontrollable
cravings. Nevertheless, our spirits work differently—when
we feed our spirits the Word of God, more worldly influ-
ences try to distract us. Conversely, if we purposely negate
spiritual nourishment, our desire to feed it diminishes.
Neglecting our spiritual staples can lead to murkiness and
darkness. If a soldier does not eat food while he or she is
on the battlefield, they will grow weak, which can result in a
physical death. If we do not communicate with the Lord and
consume the timeless gospel in the trenches, it can result
in spiritual lifelessness. So, it leads me to ask the question:
can salt lose its saltiness?

The answer can be daunting. As a compound, sodium
chloride is stable, so why would Jesus use salt as a parallel
to Christians? In the Sermon on the Mount, Jesus says, "You
are the salt of the earth; but if the salt has lost its flavor, with
what will it be salted? It is then good for nothing but to be
cast out and trodden under the feet of men" (Matt. 5:13).
Salt was used as a preservative, disinfectant, and flavor
enhancer. If any substance loses its effectiveness, it is no

good to the kingdom of God. As the Lord's Word preserves us, cleanses us, causes us to be effective witnesses of his love, grace, and power—it enables us to enhance the lives of others by adding to the building up the kingdom of God. As a seasoning, we are encouraged to help others be the very essence and savor of our Savior, thereby fulfilling our mission to enhance a flavorful aroma for the body of Christ! Jesus is saying that it is essential for believers to be the salt that preserves and flavors.

Proclamation: The world will not know about a loving Father who sent His only Son as an atonement for their sins (John 3:16) if we do not tell them. The lost, hurting, and broken should see Christ in us, the hope of glory (Col. 1:27). Losing your saltiness means losing the effectiveness of your witness to others. We have to gear up with the full armor of God (Eph. 6:11) to get out on the battlefield of life to thwart the enemies' attacks against the body of Christ—there are way too many vulnerable souls gone astray or aimlessly wandering in a spiritual desert. Our lives should make them hunger and thirst after righteousness (Matt. 5:6).

Practice: Men and women of God, please believe me when I say that your life matters. We each have a significant role in the body of Christ (Eph. 3:10,4:11,12). Those of us who are gainfully employed can, if we try, perform our duties with a smile on our faces and maintain a Godly attitude. With the help of the Holy Spirit, we can remain calm in the midst of everything going on around us and offer words of wisdom. *Our saltiness comes from Jesus, the ultimate agent of change*. He changes our hearts and cleanses our minds so we can receive His truth (II Cor. 5:17, Ezek. 36:26, Ps. 51:10). **To be salty means to be an effective agent of change.** If every church preached the truth and saints applied it to their lives, we could walk in total victory and watch more souls thirst for righteousness. How salty are *you*?

Prayer: Heavenly Father, my saltiness comes from You. You are the supreme agent of change, so empower me to be an effect agent of change. Help me to stay steadfast with feeding my spirit the Word of God so I can remain calm in the midst of disasters and misfortune all around me. I depend on Your wisdom. I pray our saltiness will cause others to thirst for Jesus. Amen.

The Cozy Church

"Not forsaking the assembling of ourselves together..."
(Hebrews 10:25).

WE LIVE IN a society that tends to be self-centered (i.e. the catch phrase "do you"), and the same characteristic can be present in a church. Whenever a local body of believers develops an inward focus on promoting themselves, ministry becomes fruitless, ineffective, and futile, which results in pacifying the flock's spiritual walk. Many believers want their church to be homey and cozy. They want to sit in the same pew near the same people, only to get upset if someone, especially a new person, takes their seat—as if their name is on it! They come to listen to a nice sermon to tickle their ears and tell them what they want to hear to get their emotional needs met—nothing convicting or a call to action. God never intended for the gathering of His people to be a form of entertainment or a social club: He calls us to join an army that will bring the gospel into enemy territory. In case you are not aware of it, there is a spiritual war going on all around us. Sitting on the sidelines is not an option – you must choose which side you will serve. Accepting Jesus as your Lord and Savior is to volunteer for His love, while rejecting Him and remaining silent, or doing nothing, puts you on the enemy's side by simple default. Neutrality does not exist.

An effective church—one that poses a real threat to the enemy—is a body of disciplined people who walk in righteousness, are learned and educated in His Word, and are skilled for service. This same church should house and train a five-fold ministry team. Ephesians 4:11-12 reads, "And he gave the apostles, the prophets, the evangelists, the shepherds and teachers, to equip the saints for the work of ministry, for building up the body of Christ." Therefore, the church should build up the believers, provide divine order, and obey God's timing and instruction. A righteous body of believers will walk in divine integrity and dedication to support others. Holy men and women of the cloth will equip and release their flock to operate in their gifts; they will not hold them back, quench the Spirit, or try to keep them bound to the church to collect their tithes and offerings. Intercessory prayer and submissive strategic movement are key to spiritual operations to show the world His remarkable love and sacrifice for His people—not for becoming a self-contained refuge of comfort.

Proclamation: The urgency of the Lord's command and the desperate condition of humanity should motivate us to leave the safety of our comfort zones and deliver the message of hope and salvation through Jesus to our families, to our neighbors, to our coworkers, to the folks in the highways and byways, to a dying world. To evade this responsibility is to miss the Father's plan for your life and the opportunity to help invest in others and build His Kingdom.

Practice: Brothers and sisters in Christ, let's not waste time or energy on trivial things and thereby miss the exciting fulfillment of God's will. He has called each one of His children, not to a life of comfortable tradition, but to an **adventure of obedience**. Are you ready and willing to listen to the Lord? Are you going to answer His call? Which side are you on? Remember, you cannot be neutral. Sign up—you'll help achieve the great commission and fill His kingdom with people from every tribe and nation.

Prayer: Heavenly Father, I am ready for my adventure of obedience! I realize we are at war in the spirit. Use me to reach Your various tribes and nations. I will no longer sit on the sidelines, concerned with my own comfort. I choose YOU, Lord. Here I am, Father; send me. Amen.

The Road to Freedom

I walk the streets
Despite the tweets
Nevertheless,
I fall into a dark hole,
Feeling like a lost soul...
I get up out
With a great shout.
I walk down the same streets
With the same tweets
Yet I slip into the same hole
Once again losing control...
This time I emerge
Like I'm on the verge
Of something big.

Trying to beat the same streets
With the same tweets
With my eyes open wide
Increasing my stride...
Right into the same hole
Learning my role
With a humble attitude
Finding gratitude
For a Mighty Savior
Who has found favor
On me
In my mess
Struggling to pass the test
Tired of being bound
Breaking foul ground.

Thrive!

Without skipping a beat
I find a new street
Looking for something new
Not fake, but true...
Breaking the chains
No more restraints
Receiving instructions from above
To stroll in love—
Feel me?

CPSIA information can be obtained
at www.ICGtesting.com
Printed in the USA
LVHW020910210920
666634LV00002B/189

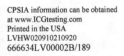

9 781631 298752